Library and Archives Canada
Cataloguing in Publication

Moriyama, Raymond
The legacy document :
Canadian War Museum /
Raymond Moriyama.

Issued also in French under title:
Document fondateur,
Musée canadien de la guerre.
ISBN 978-0-660-03398-3
Cat. no.: NM44-1/2015E

1. Canadian War Museum.
2. Military museums – Ontario – Ottawa – Design and construction.
3. Museum architecture – Ontario – Ottawa.

I. Canadian War Museum.
II. Title.
III. Title: Canadian War Museum.

U13 C32O89 2015
355.0074'71384
C2015-980048-X

Published by the
Canadian War Museum
1 Vimy Place
Ottawa, ON K1A 0M8
warmuseum.ca

Printed and bound in Canada.

lest we forget
CANADIAN WAR MUSEUM
MUSÉE CANADIEN DE LA GUERRE
CANADA
n' oublions jamais

THE LEGACY DOCUMENT: CANADIAN WAR MUSEUM

RAYMOND MORIYAMA

POSTSCRIPT

Having happily sent the final copy of the Legacy Document to a printer and binder, I discovered at the eleventh hour that it would be possible to insert two final pages into the document, which I am writing a few weeks after completing the Legacy Document assignment.

I have just finished a successful two-stage adjudication of the National Holocaust Monument Competition in Ottawa with an uncommonly devoted jury of diverse backgrounds and deep understanding of the Holocaust.

I write firstly because the site of the Monument is adjacent to the Canadian War Museum, and at an important entry point into Ottawa and the Parliamentary Precinct at the northeast corner of Booth and Wellington Streets.

Although there were many outstanding ideas and sensitivities in the other five submissions, I write because the winning concept, if carried out as its potential indicates, will put Ottawa and Canada on the international map of Holocaust monuments and memorials that all Jewish communities worldwide will bow to and that Canadians could be very proud of.

The decision of the jury was unanimous.

I write because the winning design concept is a beautiful balance and counterpoint to the Canadian War Museum, conceptually, spiritually and architecturally.

I write because a physical link between the War Museum and the National Holocaust Monument will not only enhance each of them, but will raise each's significance and stature without affecting their purpose and objectives.

I write because the expansion of the War Museum that we have previously discussed, studied and proposed requires insertion of other factors and greater convergence of subtleties, clarity and boldness. What it means is that the future expansion of the War Museum under Booth Street and to the east side of Booth is now necessary to truly make the link between the National Holocaust Monument and the Museum.

Now a clear mandate is required to negotiate the easterly site for the Museum's expansion.

What an amazing coincidence of time, space, forms and experiences of two major projects in Canada coming together.

Please insure the path to greatness is assured.

Raymond Moriyama
27/02/14

CONTENTS

FOREWORD

By Mark O'Neill
President and Chief Executive Officer
Canadian Museum of History

Since its opening to the public on May 8, 2005, the 60th anniversary of VE Day, the Canadian War Museum has become a recognizable icon on its prominent location near the Ottawa River, just a few kilometres from Parliament Hill. The building was an instant success and, over the years, has become a recognizable destination for Canadians and visitors to Canada wishing to understand how war history has shaped our country, while marveling at the building's architectural symbolism.

As President and Chief Executive Officer of the Canadian Museum of History and former Director General of the Canadian War Museum, I proudly endorse this Legacy Document prepared by the War Museum's Principal Design Architect, Raymond Moriyama. This remarkable commentary on the design principles of the building will help the Museum to meet the dual challenges of safeguarding Mr. Moriyama's vision and ensuring that any changes to the building continue to support its mandate and functions.

This Legacy Document is intended as a permanent reference for the conservation of the building and its setting. It can be used to clarify the original design intent, to manage proposals for change and to influence planning directions for the site and for adjacent sites and sightlines.

It is my hope that this publication will serve as a model to be followed by other organizations, ensuring that generations to come are properly informed about the vision and guiding design principles behind Canada's great architectural buildings.

ASSIGNMENT

By Guy Larocque
Director, Facility Management
Canadian Museum of History

THE REQUEST TO THE ORIGINAL ARCHITECT

Inspired by a visit to Sydney Australia's Opera House designed by Jorn Utzon, I approached Raymond Moriyama to ask if he would be interested in producing a Legacy Document of Design Principles for the Canadian War Museum. The design principles set out in such legacy documents are to be used continuously over time as a guide to facility managers, exhibition designers and organization leaders in making decisions when changes to buildings are being contemplated as part of the organization's evolution over time.

THE VISION

In order for this legacy document to be successful, it is important for future designers to understand what inspired the Principle Design Architect's vision. This will provide any future designers with a starting point from which they could then study the building and thus be given the opportunity to comprehend how the Principle Design Architect's original vision is expressed in the building's forms and functions. This understanding is fundamental to maintaining the integrity of the original vision and allows that vision to carry through into any contemplated design changes.

Therefore, the first task in this assignment to Raymond Moriyama was to ask him to describe what inspired his vision for the building and how he arrived at the architectural theme for the building and its site. Then, he was asked to explain how the design came about, what lead eventually to the design concept and the relationship of the building to its surroundings. Finally, Raymond Moriyama was asked to complete the outline of his vision with a statement about the essence of the vision.

THE FUTURE

A large, multi-function building such as the Canadian War Museum will undergo many natural changes over time. As organizational needs change, so will there be a need to modify the building to suit the operational functions and technologies of the day.

This section of the Legacy Document should describe the approach by which future changes to the building are to be undertaken to maintain the character of the original design. Therefore, it is important that Raymond Moriyama record in this section of the Legacy Document what characteristics of the building need to be respected to maintain such important features as the site lines from outside and within the building, the general look and feel of the building's shapes and materials, and the preservation of key architectural elements without which the essence of the building's image could be irreparably harmed. This section of the Legacy Document should also include a description of the architectural elements that unfortunately did not survive through to construction and that were very much a part of the original vision.

THE DESIGN PRINCIPLES

This section of the Legacy Document is where the Principle Design Architect may establish a clear set of principles for managing future design changes for the Canadian War Museum. His comments are expected to be made in the context of his understanding of the Canadian War Museum's current and future needs.

In this section, the Principle Design Architect should present the objectives and intent of the design principles and his views on why the building design matters. Fundamental design principles would then be presented in greater detail to guide future designers on environmental sustainability, building form, orientation, materiality, light, colour and Raymond Moriyama's trademark "human scale."

This building also harbours very unique and original spaces whose design principles should be presented separately, such as Memorial Hall, Regeneration Hall, the 11/11/11 sun angle, the concrete structure and the accessible green roof.

Finally, the design principles should contain the Project Design Architect's recommendations on the planning approach for the process of maintaining the original vision and design principles.

OTHER REQUIREMENTS

Because images are so fundamental in describing what words cannot in communicating a vision and in conveying the design principles for a building, the Legacy Document should contain original sketches, design drafts, photos, etc., that would be useful in adding clarity and understanding to future users of this Document.

It is understood that any of Raymond Moriyama's associates who contribute to the production of this Legacy Document will be given due credit.

INTRODUCTION

By Raymond Moriyama

What a great honour, as the original project and design leader of the Canadian War Museum, to be requested to write this Legacy Document.

Each member of the design and construction team worked diligently and extremely hard from the inception of the project through to completion, many with extraordinary passion and dedication. The entire process was a challenging race against the clock: a fast-tracked project-delivery method and a construction management system with countless invisible behind-the-scenes activities to overcome. The architecture itself was neither straightforward nor easily understood, and the vision as well as the approach to achieving it were foreign to many of the senior client representatives. The inherent formal logic was also complex, as the concept and architecture were responding to the abundance of Canadian voices: often abstract, sometimes vague, mostly seeking a modest, sustainable, inexpensive yet courageous and truly Canadian architectural solution. Thus, I am extremely happy, eager and proud to carry out the task of explaining the Vision, the Future and the Design Principles of the Canadian War Museum, so as to clarify the architecture and to outline certain aspects of the building that must be completed and others that must be maintained to preserve the institutional vision and the architectural integrity now and into the future.

I intend this Legacy Document to be useful — a living document, a reference and constant guide for all those involved in administration, maintenance and further future development, renovations and additions.

Having a Legacy Document does not imply any physical architectural changes. Far from it. This document is intended to encourage updating and future thinking, while keeping in mind the original vision, concept and purpose of serving visitors and Canadians alike before proceeding with any ad-hoc or improvised changes or alterations to meet new needs and new technologies. The updating of services, such as mechanical, plumbing, electrical, security and civil works, is implicit and is not a part of this assignment.

This document is divided into three distinct sections:

1. The Background: an introductory history of the inception of the Canadian War Museum and the story of how our team was awarded the project.
2. Detailed instructions on the current and future steps that will help maintain the design integrity of the building.
3. A look to the future, and a gesture of hope.

THE BACKGROUND

SCHEDULING AND CONTROL OF TIME

Many years of discussions had taken place over the need for a new war museum. These discussions were documented and form valuable background material for understanding the Canadian War Museum and this Legacy Document.

In 2000, the decision to proceed with the War Museum was finally made with the chief mandate: "Educate, Preserve, Remember." A proposal call for architects was announced. The location for the new museum was to be the site adjacent to the Canadian Aviation and Space Museum. The location was expansive and easily capable of accommodating any architectural program and physical requirements, but the site was some distance from the city centre and many of Ottawa's tourist attractions.

For many years I had the intention of forming a Joint Venture with Griffith Rankin Cook (GRC) of Ottawa when "the right, perfect project came along." After two decades of discussions with Alex Rankin, this Proposal Call for the War Museum Project was 'IT.' The project felt perfect for our collaboration.

We worked very hard on our submission. We submitted the proposal from Toronto where the courier promised on a stack of bibles to deliver the submission in Ottawa before the deadline.

The courier missed the deadline by a few minutes, and our submission was rightly rejected!

The team was stunned and devastated. I was mentally crushed and bit my tongue at the crude reason given by the courier for missing the deadline: "It was the snow," as if we do not have snow in Canadian winters!

It took me months to get over this disappointment. But I could not stop thinking about the project, asking questions such as:

- How can architects surpass the "Educate, Preserve, Remember" mandate?
- How should they express a national war museum in Ottawa?
- How could the museum express Canadians?
- What would the voices of Canadians say?
- What influence would they have on the vision and the concept?
- What are the other factors that could influence the design?

Fortune was smiling on us; heaven, too, was feeling my passion.

The Prime Minister at the time, Jean Chrétien, who was interested in architecture as a career in his youth, changed the location of the project to a more central and accessible site, just west of the Parliamentary Precinct. This move cancelled not only the previously committed site; it also forced a new proposal call for architects.

This time, with greater optimism, more thoughts about Canadians and the uniqueness of Canada, and much greater belief in ourselves, we worked even harder. Rather than rely on a courier, my son, Ajon, drove from Toronto to deliver the second proposal. I was relieved, even ecstatic, when he phoned from Ottawa happily announcing that the Joint Venture Team package was delivered before the deadline.

We were shortlisted together with several other teams for the second phase of the selection process. I was confident we could win, but we worked feverishly on this second submission to prove our worth.

Finally, we were asked with, I believe, four other teams to attend an interview by the Architects Selection Committee on October 16, 2001.

Prior to this date, my son Jason and I spent several days in the offices of GRC in Ottawa and jointly with Alex Rankin refined a PowerPoint presentation, clarifying our objectives, budget, organization and approach to design and construction, and simplifying our communication to the Committee. They were hard working days, but we were exhilarated by the emerging awareness that GRC and Moriyama & Teshima (MTA) shared a common spirit, attitude and dedication to the pursuit of excellence and the search for the soul of the War Museum's design solution.

The interview took place in the Boardroom of the Canadian Museum of Civilization (now the Canadian Museum of History). Five of us were allowed to attend. Following a relaxing introduction of our five members and the committee members, we positioned a placemat, much like the ones in a good restaurant, in front of each interviewer outlining our agenda and the items on the agenda. A tightly organized, perfectly timed and choreographed PowerPoint presentation followed the agenda items.

ITEMS LISTED ON THE PLACEMAT

Key Project Team Member Roles:
Raymond Moriyama: Partner-in-charge
Alex Rankin: Back-up Partner
Jason Moriyama: Project Architect
John Cook: Project Administrator
Don Cruikshank: TMP Mechanical Partner

PLACEMAT AGENDA

List of the complete Team
Organization of Project including the Client
Approach to Design
Research
Budget
Schedule

The interview was stimulating. The questions asked by the Committee Members were all brilliant. I believe we answered all of them simply, straightforwardly and honestly. It helped that we immediately liked all the members of the Committee. I was happy with the interview.

And as the saying goes: "The rest is history!"

The Canadian War Museum Project officially started on November 1, 2001, and the Grand Opening took place on the 60th Anniversary of VE Day: May 8, 2005, and included the completion and opening of all exhibits.

Thus began a remarkable Joint Venture of GRC and MTA that, I believe, was forged in heaven. Even more exceptional was the bonding of two individuals — Alex Rankin and myself, Raymond Moriyama.

The completion of the building had to be nearly six months prior to the official opening to allow time for exhibit installation. That gave us, the architectural team, a total window for research, design, contract documentation and construction of three and half years: a very aggressive and ambitious schedule for a major national museum and an institution of over 40,000 square metres.

We had no time to visit other war museums, which I applauded. Instead, I insisted as we had stated in our presentation that we listen to the voices of Canadians across our nation to learn what Canadians think and feel about war and a new war museum. Although I was passionate about the project, I was personally determined to resign from the project if the reactions of Canadians across Canada were negative to the idea of a new Canadian War Museum.

Aside from my Chancellorship at Brock University, I dedicated myself totally to this one single project. The Canadian War Musuem was to be my last architectural project before retirement.

A FEW OF THE DESIGN TEAM MEMBERS AT THE SITE, CIRCA WINTER 2004

DIARMUID NASH, RAYMOND MORIYAMA, MTA, ALEX RANKIN, GRC.

JASON MORIYAMA

EARL RENKE

BRIAN RUDY

LOUIS LORTIE

ALEX LEUNG

THE VISION

Every architect has his or her personal motivation and/or vision for a project.

THE MOTIVATION

My motivation was to create a war museum that is an expression of the wishes and vision of the Canadians with whom we met, and to carry it out under budget and on time for the official opening.

THE TWO MAJOR INFLUENCES

For this project, two sources that exerted major influences on my vision were both related to sounds.

The first sound was the sound of nature: a breeze over an imagined battlefield, at night to be exact.

I made a remarkable discovery of myself on my first visit to the site. A profound experience I had when I was 13 years old resurfaced 60 years later to inspire the first vision of this project. It was the sound of a mystical breeze that I heard as I was suspended in my tree house, which I had built alone, secretly, in the Rockies, in desperation, in the internment camp that I was living in at the time. One dark evening the sound of the breeze filtering through the tree house created images of war in my mind.

TREE HOUSE IN INTERNMENT CAMP, CIRCA 1943

The sound was so acute, I could envision soldiers on both sides resting in the dark for a few hours — wet, cold, dirty, hungry, full of fear with death all around them and wishing the madness would subside. Hope! Peace! This haunting sound of nature surfaced 60 years later from some deep crevasses of my mind and heart. The first sketch of the War Museum that I drew was not an image of a physical thing, but one of nature's sound as it re-awakened within me — and with it, a feeling of war.

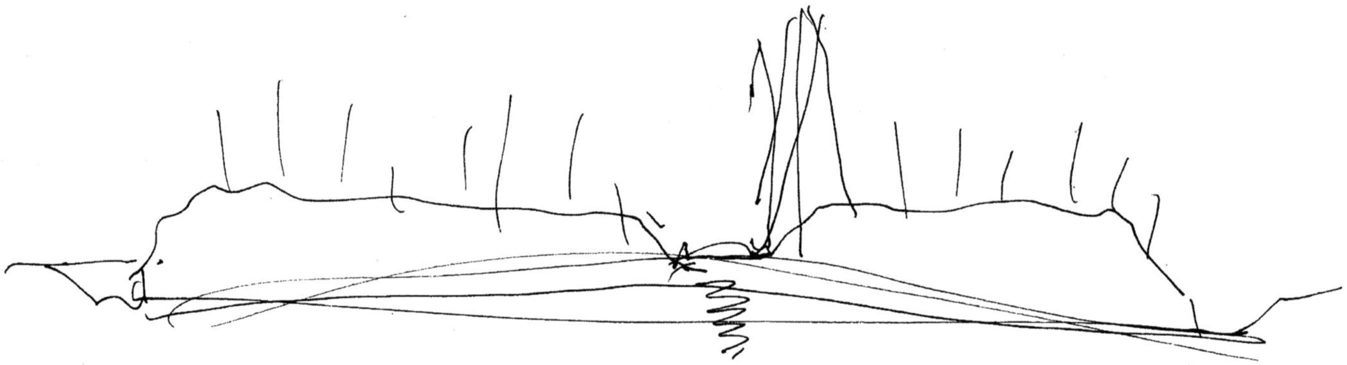

The second was the sound of human voices — of Canadians across the nation expressing innermost thoughts about war and a war museum for Canada. These I had the honour of hearing with Joe Geurts, the Director of the Canadian War Museum at the time.

Thoughts and opinions varied vastly between men and women.

Men were mainly earthy, macho, yet modest, and spoke of "good times and bad times" and "personal experiences." Words like "gallant," "bravery," "unselfish" and "chivalry" were common. No man questioned his allegiance to Canada. They also offered advice such as "keep the cost down" and "give us good design to be proud of, but at a modest cost."

ABOVE: THE INITIAL SKETCH OF THE VISION — SOUND OF NATURE

Women, I found, were gentle, strong and spoke of universal thoughts such as "war is like going to the depth of hell to resurrect the soul." There was less of "us and them."

"When I walked across Beaumont Hamel after the war and after reaching the other side, I looked down. My boots were covered with red mud. I shuddered. If it had been just after the battles when over 700 Newfoundlanders were killed or maimed, my boots would have been covered with blood — and Newfoundland was not even a part of Canada." One wise lady advised me, "an impeccable architect gives up a part of his ego to embody the soul of the nation he serves." Then my question was "what is the soul of Canada?" That question has remained with me to this day, and continues to inform my views on every new piece of architecture erected in this country.

The sound of nature intertwined with the voices of Canadians was the initial inspiration. Naturally, poems seemed to enter the realm of sounds and, of course, music — Wagner's sober operas, the swings of the Forties playing in airplane hangars — Glen Miller, Tommy Dorsey, Lionel Hampton, Stan Kenton — the exciting early jazz of the Twenties with Louis Armstrong among many. They all came into a mix of wartime sound.

Stirring in my heart was an insatiable need to create an architecture that was more than just a contemporary museum container sheltering the exhibits, tanks and wartime armories. The architecture itself had to embody a Canadian soul and to have a direct role as an exhibit of war. The Vision of sounds together with many other influences emerged as an architectural concept of '"Regenerative Landscape."

THE SITE BEFORE

THE SITE AFTER

THE OTHER INFLUENCES

The site west of the Parliamentary Precinct and downtown Ottawa made the War Museum much more accessible to the general public. Albeit smaller than the first site, it had the Ottawa River and the Riverside Canada Trail to the north, a wonderful view of the river, the island and Gatineau, and the amazing sounds of the Ottawa River and the Chaudière Falls.

The view of Gatineau and the province of Quebec kept whispering some idea in my brain. The Parliamentary Precinct and the Peace Tower offered a connection that helped to inform the design, and act as physical connectors to the essence of Canadian democracy.

THE SITE CONDITIONS

We soon found many challenging physical site conditions:

1. The site, an original industrial section of Ottawa, was totally contaminated. The Fire of 1900 destroyed this area, together with one-fifth of the entire city.

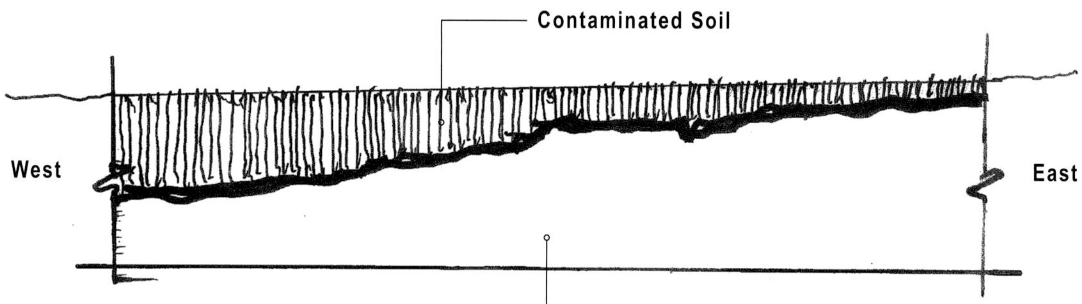

SECTION OF SITE

2. A solid rock ledge underground occurred from a shallow one metre below grade at the east end, sloping deeper toward the west end.
3. The site was flood-prone.
4. The site was in an earthquake zone.

Solving these conditions economically and quickly was a challenge.

THE OTHER INTRIGUING CONDITIONS THAT MADE THEIR WAY INTO THE DESIGN

The Peace Tower: a symbol of our Canadian democracy is directly to the east of the site.

The constructed urban environment to the east and the pastoral landscape to the west intersected at the Museum site. The architecture of the Museum needed to embrace these two conditions genteelly and elegantly.

THE CANADIAN SENSIBILITY

As stated earlier, my motivation was to create a distinctively unique Canadian War Museum that reflects Canadian sensibility about war and the war museum at a minimal cost and on time for the official opening on May 8, 2005.

I was determined to express the exceptional thoughts and input that we received as the key to the clarity of the Vision of the War Museum. I was not surprised by the gentleness and the thoughtfulness of the comments, which were very Canadian in their modesty yet strong in clarity of belief. Voices were anti-war, not anti-heroes, and in favour of a new museum with a Canadian expression and sensibility that appealed to both women and men alike. Several women commented that the old war museum was despised for its male-oriented approach.

REMEMBRANCE DAY AT 11:00 A.M.

Remembrance Day, November 11 at 11:00 a.m. is one moment at which all Canadians are united in silence to honour those who served Canada and the world in pursuit of peace. "Lest We Forget."

THE HONOUR AND HOPE

The Canadian War Museum was and is intended to preserve and honour our past, our Canadian bravery and sacrifices. It also expresses the future, the hope for peace. This dual-purpose was raised at many of the interviews that we conducted during our research. The question was how to consolidate these two ideas together architecturally in one building. Architecture surely needs to be a part of the exhibits, not just a passive container or a rigorous defender of wars.

RIGHT: SELECTED SAMPLES OF THE 64 THEMES AND MODELS STUDIED

THE CONCEPT

THE 64 ALTERNATIVE THEMES AND DESIGNS

We explored various themes and ideas through the creation of 64 concept designs, each with its own physical model.

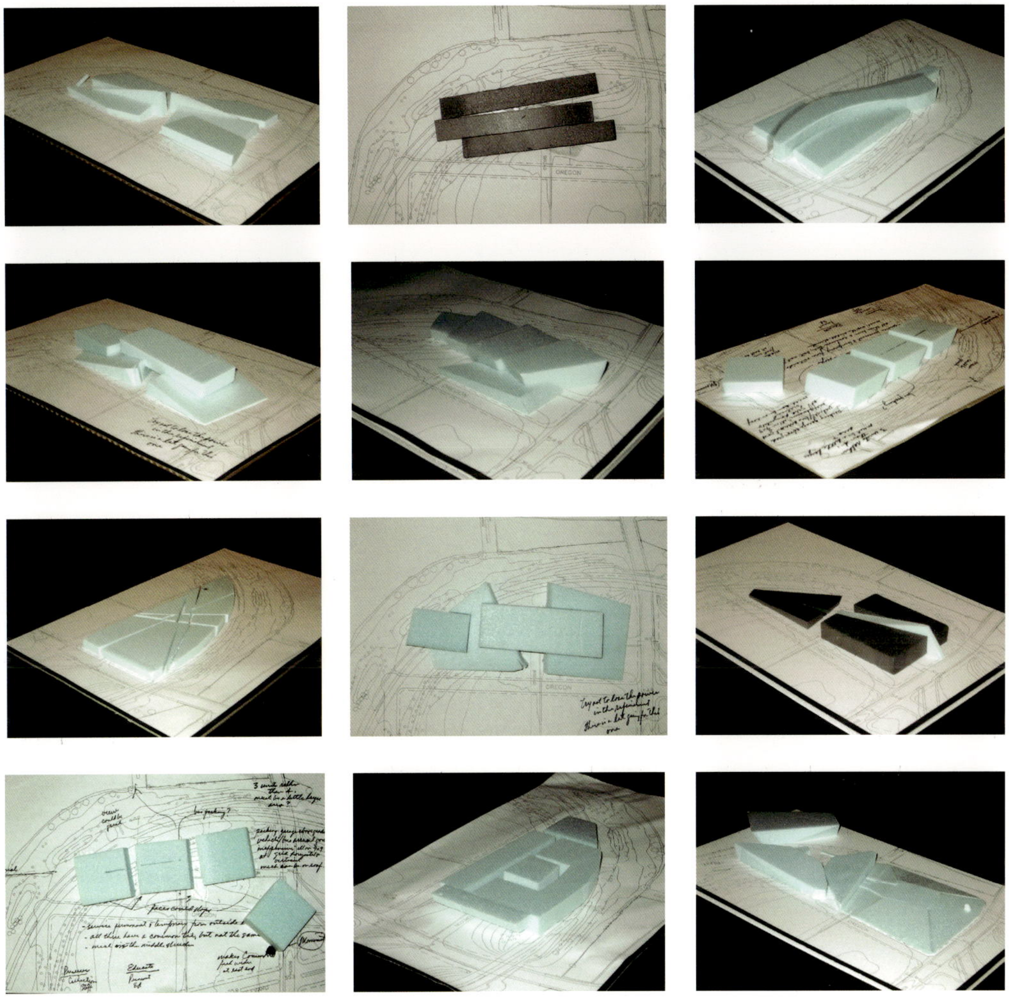

THE FINAL THREE DESIGNS

After GRC and MTA narrowed the alternatives down to 12, Joe Geurts and the client committee, together with our team representatives, further reduced them to three options. These three options were fully developed as Schematic Designs, each one under a separate team — one team under Jason Moriyama, another under Diarmuid Nash and the third under myself. These designs were placed on a national website for public input. In two weeks, the client received over 1,200 comments and, based on those, the Board cast its final vote.

The winning design was further refined and put on a fast-track schedule.

I was still planning to resign if the anti-war museum vote was more than 10%. It was 4%, which meant that there was astounding support for the project.

RIGHT: THE FINAL THREE DESIGNS PLACED ON NATIONAL WEB SITE

THE INFLUENCES

THE CANADIAN LANDSCAPE COAST TO COAST

The design was influenced by the Canadian landscape from the East Coast to the West Coast, including the Maritimes, rolling Quebec and Ontario, the Prairies, the Foothills, the Rockies and the West Coast.

THE POEMS OF WAR

Poems of war were great influences. Here are two examples.

"Grass" by Carl Sandburg.
Pile the bodies high at Austerlitz and Waterloo.
Shovel them under and let me work—
I am the grass; I cover all.
And pile them high at Gettysburg
And pile them high at Ypres and Verdun.
Shovel them under and let me work.
Two years, ten years, and passengers ask the conductor:
What place is this?
Where are we now?
I am the grass.
Let me work.

"Memorial Tablet" by Siegfried Sassoon.
... I died in hell—
(They called it Passchendaele). My wound was slight,
And I was hobbling back; and then a shell
Burst slick upon the duck-boards: so I fell
Into the bottomless mud, and lost the light.

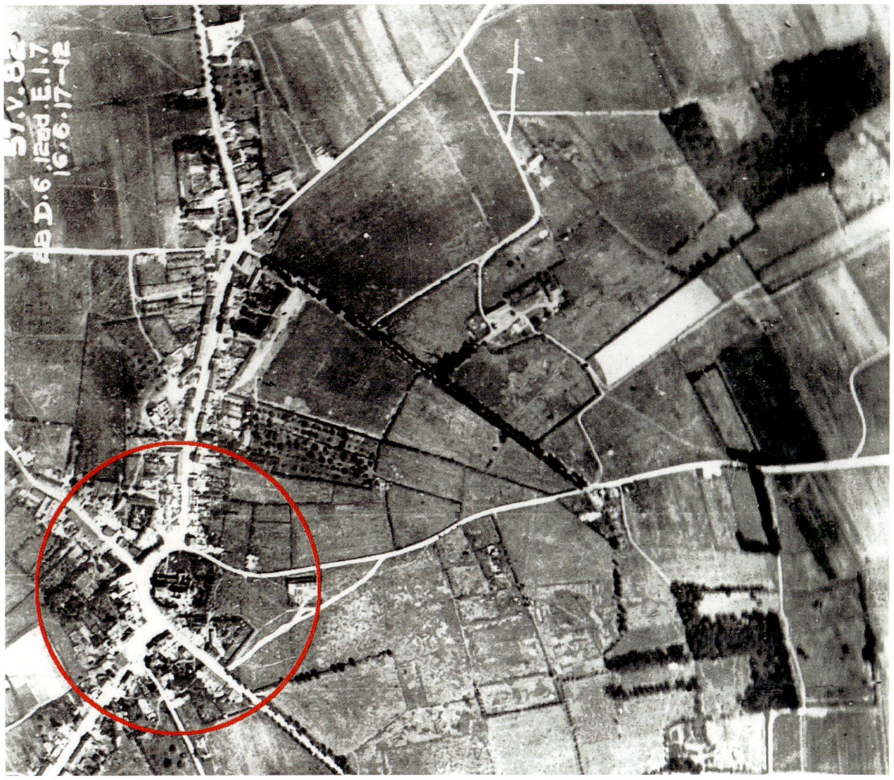
57.V.82
16.6.17–12

THE PAINTINGS OF WAR

Paintings of war by Canadian artists moved us greatly. Here are only a few examples from the War Museum's collection, which is of inestimable value.

THE STORIES OF NEWFOUNDLANDERS AT BEAUMONT HAMEL

The design was also influenced by stories of battles at Beaumont Hamel and the bravery of Newfoundlanders before Newfoundland joined Canada as a province.

THE RELATIONSHIP TO THE SITE

The design was also informed by the relationship of the site to the built and natural contexts, such as:

THE PEACE TOWER

THE PASTORIAL OTTAWA WEST

THE URBAN OTTAWA EAST

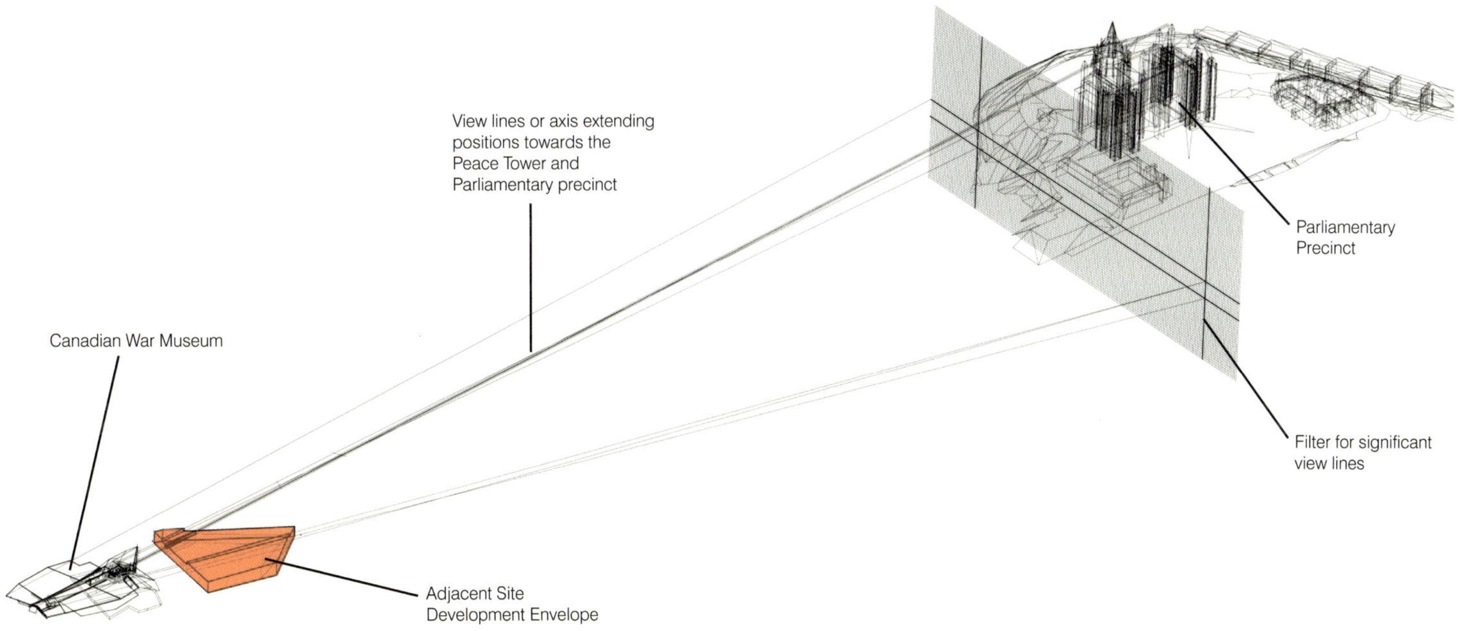

Careful consideration was given to:

THE SIGNIFICANCE OF THE QUEBEC–ONTARIO BORDER

THE ISLAND AND CHAUDIÈRE FALLS

The island is significant for its history as the beginning of Canada, the Aboriginal nations and the famous "unseen" Chaudière Falls.

THE NCC PLANS FOR THE AREA AROUND THE SITE

Especially to the south:

THE CEREMONIAL ROUTE

The Ceremonial Route runs along the east side of the site on Booth Street.

THE AXIS OF THE SUN PRECISELY AT 11/11/11

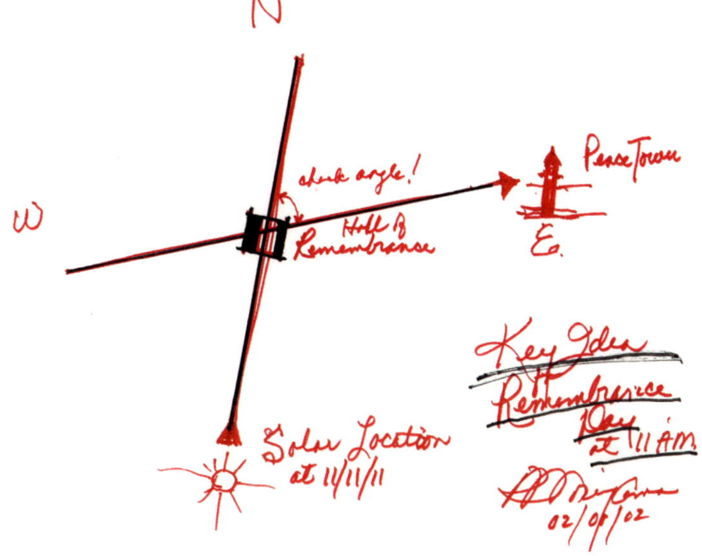

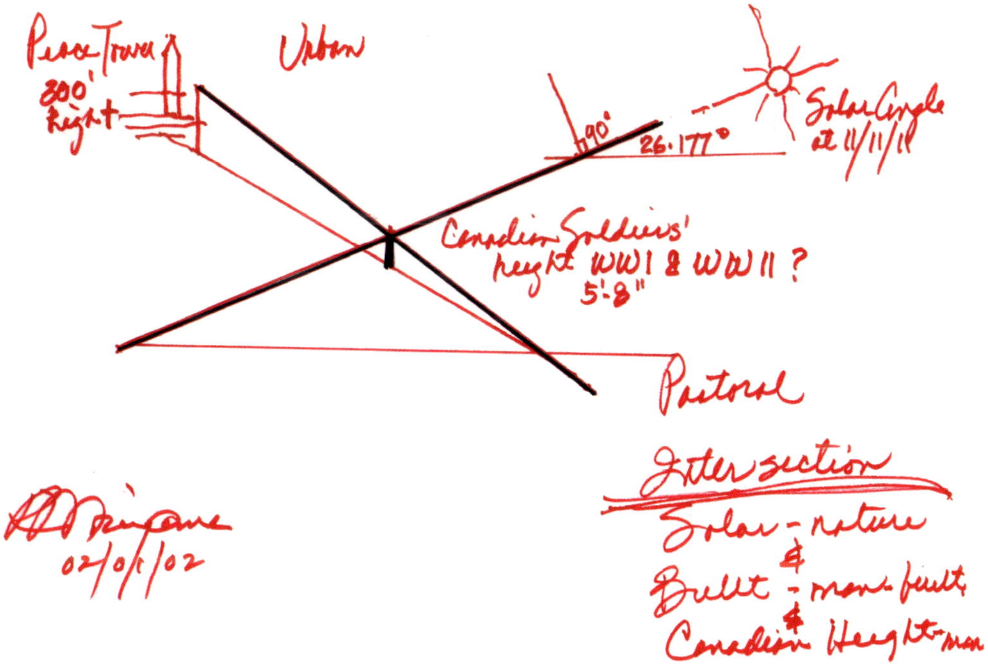

THE SELF-IMPOSED BUDGET

On our Canadian tour, we were often told to create "good design, but make it economical."

"Don't spend too much money, but make it great."

Result: Our team established a very frugal budget for this national museum — two-thirds of other museums such as the National Gallery (updated cost: $350.00 per square foot) and the Canadian Museum of Civilization (also $350.00 per square foot). My intention was to be under $234.00 per square foot. Final cost received from the Project Manager of the Contractor was $218.00 per square foot, $16.00 per square foot lower than my budget or 62.2% of the cost for the Museum of Civilization and the National Gallery.

THE IMPORTANCE OF SUSTAINABILITY

"Make the museum energy efficient."

RESULTING DESIGN: A COMPACT BUILDING PLAN

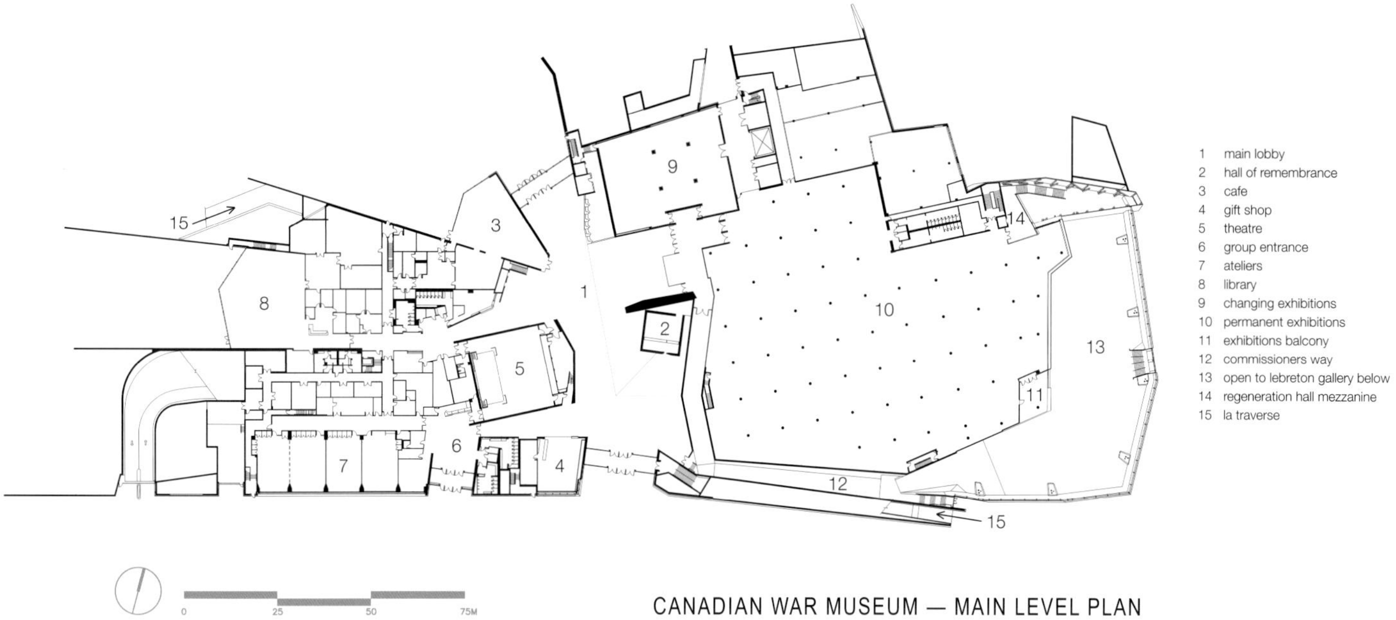

CANADIAN WAR MUSEUM — MAIN LEVEL PLAN

DENSE CONCRETE

The walls are built of dense concrete, increasing the building's thermal mass.

THE MAJOR PARTS OF THE BUILDING ARE BELOW GRADE

And the walls are protected weather-wise by cover of earth.

THE LOW PROFILE

The profile of the Museum is designed with prevailing winter winds from the northwest in mind. The west end of the Museum is only a few metres above grade and rises slowly to the east, so as not to interrupt wind patterns.

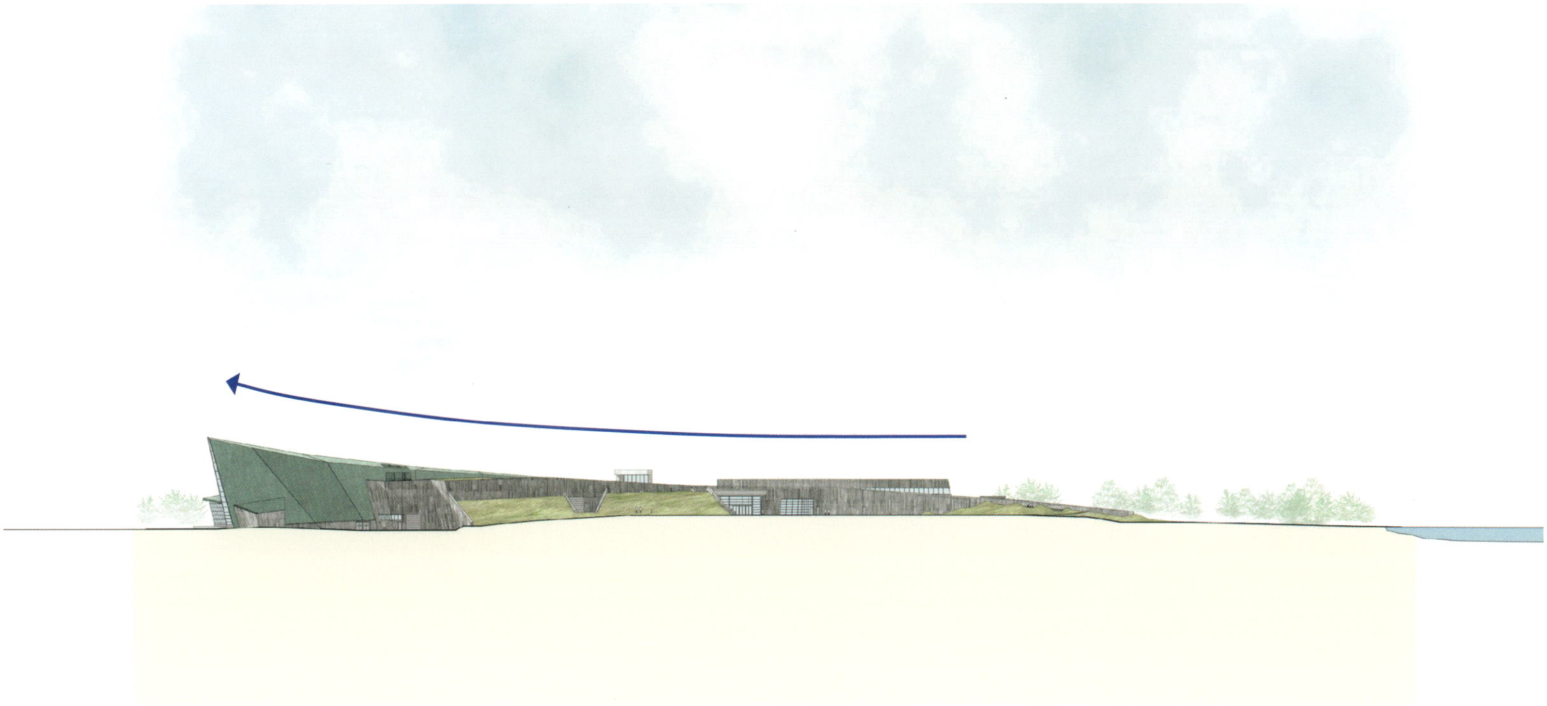

PREVAILING WINTER WIND

THE EARTH- AND PLANT-COVERED GREEN ROOF

THE SMALL GLAZING AREA FACING PREVAILING WINTER WINDS

Limited, thermopane glazing faces the prevailing winter winds.

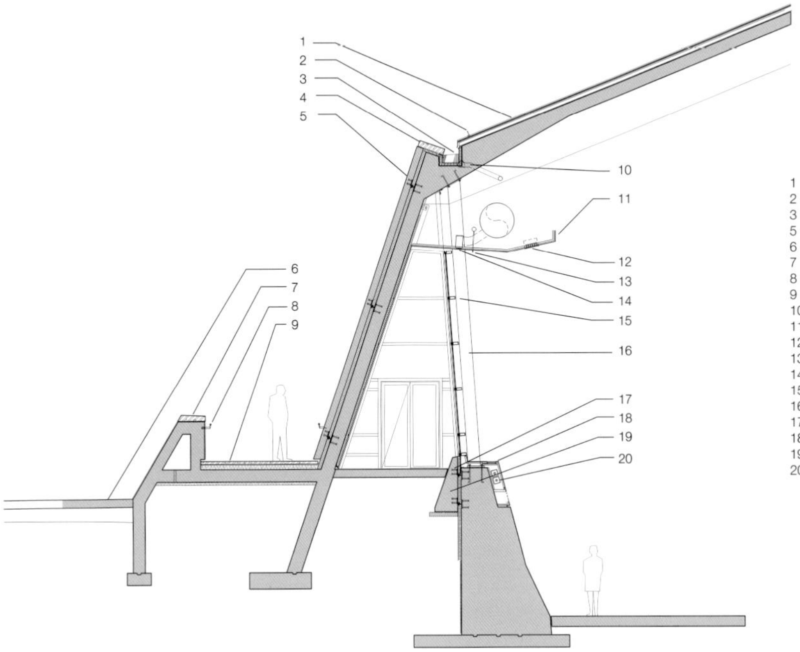

1 standing seam copper roof
2 snow fence
3 pvc liner in formed concrete gutter
5 site cast poured in place concrete cladding
6 concrete sidewalk
7 precast concrete coping
8 painted steel handrail
9 precast concrete unit paving
10 scupper drain
11 suspended gypsum board ceiling
12 recessed lighting
13 sprinkler
14 supply air linear diffuser
15 double glazing in aluminum curtain wall framing
16 painted steel wind column beyond
17 site cast ancors
18 break formed hot rolled steel radiator cover
19 site cast poured in place concrete cladding
20 hot water radiator

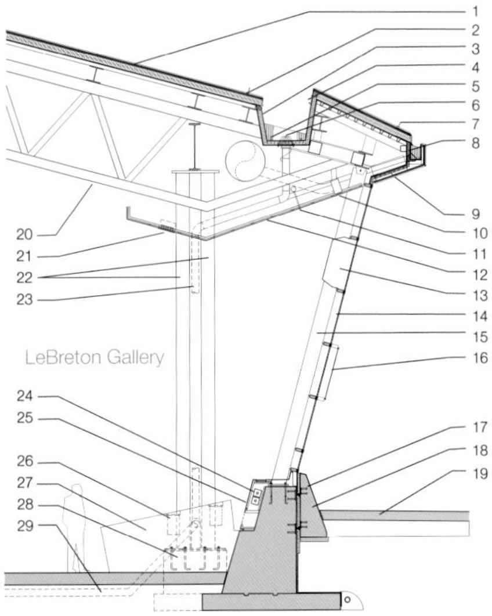

1 standing seam copper roof
2 snow fence
3 sheet metal on formed steel gutter
4 safety anchor line
5 de-icing cable
6 roof drain
7 standing seam copper roof
8 pvc liner on formed steel gutter
9 standing seam copper soffit
10 supply air linear diffuser
11 sprinkler
12 suspended gypsum board ceiling
13 prefinished sheet metal shadow box
14 double glazing in aluminum curtain wall framing
15 painted steel wind column beyond
16 suspended fritted glass panel
17 site cast ancors
18 site cast poured in place concrete cladding
19 concrete sidewalk
20 painted structural steel truss
21 recessed lighting
22 painted steel columns beyond
23 painted steel rain leader column
24 hot water radiator
25 break formed hot rolled steel radiator cover
26 recessed uplight
27 poured in place concrete column base beyond
28 structural column base
29 under slab strom line

DETAILED WALL SECTION THROUGH LEBRETON GALLERY

0 1 2 3 4 5M

"AN IMPECCABLE ARCHITECT"

TO BE A MOON NOT THE SUN

A number of quotes that I mentioned previously ended up finding physical form in the building: "An impeccable architect gives up a part of his ego to embody the soul of the nation he serves." This statement from a wise lady made a strong impact on my role as a principle architect on the project. The design reflects the thoughts, ideas, feeling and premonitions of Canadians. If Canadians were to be the sun, I tried to be the moon, bathed in sunlight, but reflecting a clearer a more obvious, integrated reflection of the thoughts.

Another statement from an equally wise woman was "War is like going to the depth of hell to resurrect the soul."

The result of this statement is reflected in the design of the Entrance Foyer.

I originally wanted to dip the Entrance Foyer downward to literally reflect the statement, "like going to the depth of hell," but the rock ledge below grade and my determination not to use dynamite in earthquake-prone Ottawa forced a solution that "heaved" the floor and ceiling up and down, set to the darkness of Wagner's opera and the power of the absence of light.

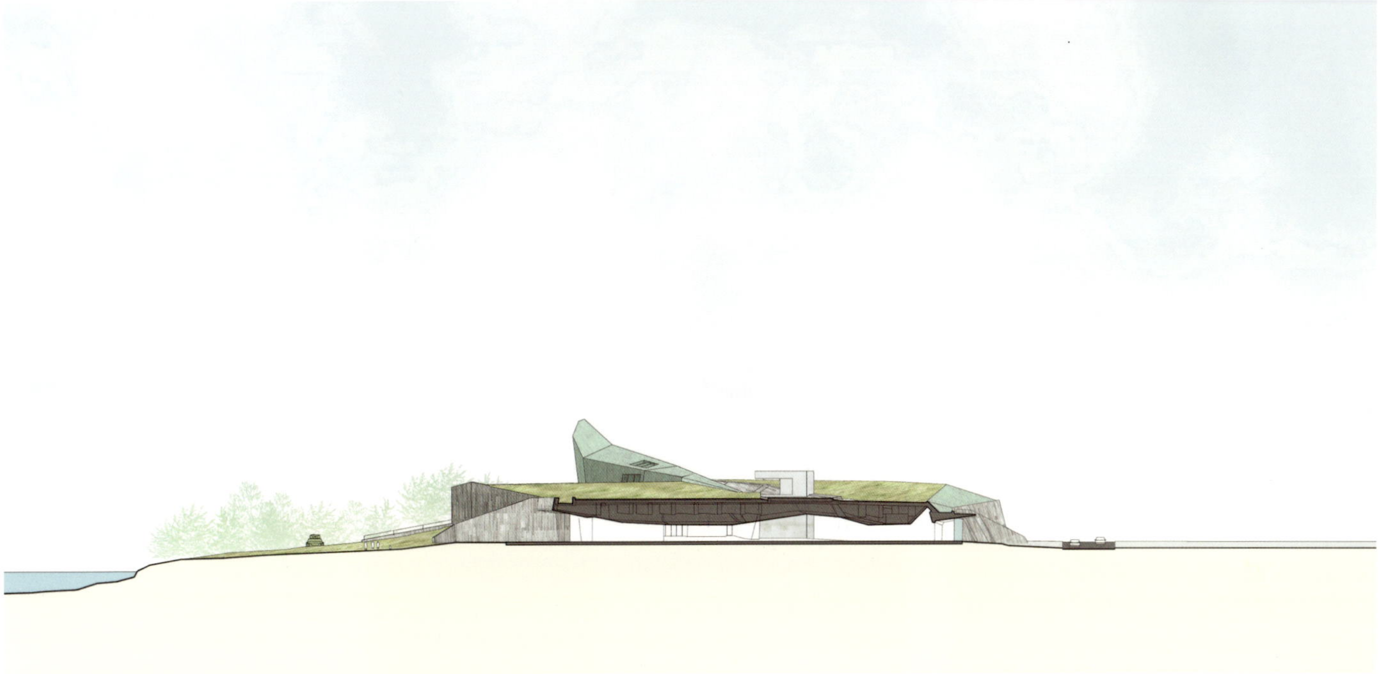

"We must respect and honour those Canadians who served our country and preserved our way of life."

Result: Memorial Hall or the Hall of Remembrance as I like to call it. The space is exactly 9m x 9m x 9m.

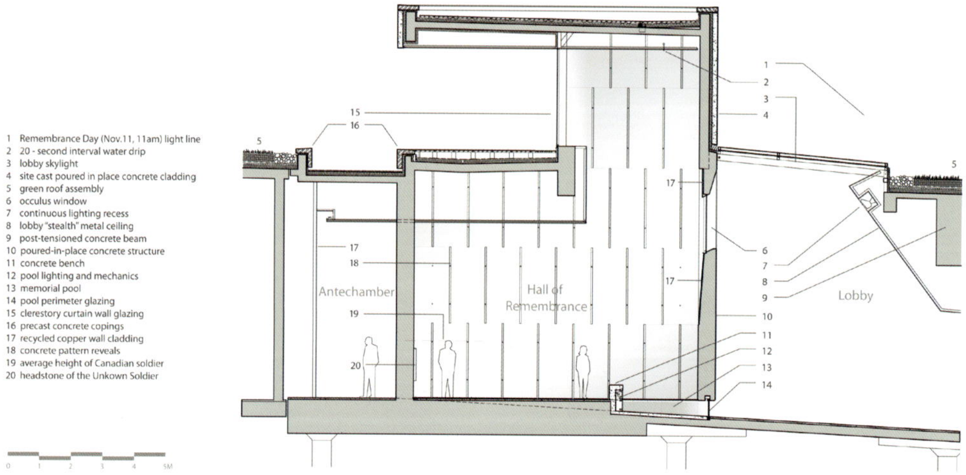

DETAILED WALL SECTION THROUGH HALL OF REMEMBRANCE

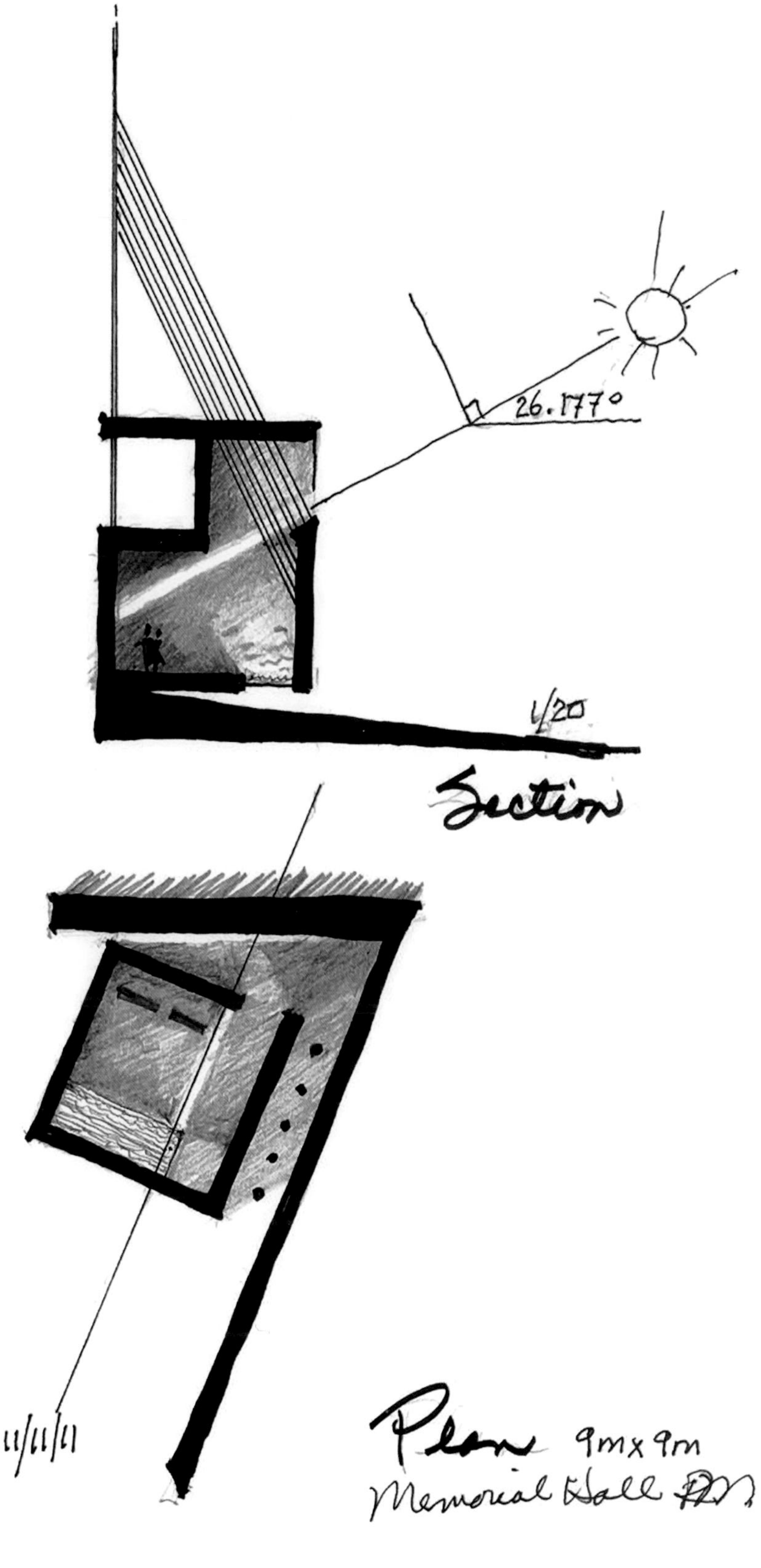
26.177°
1/20
Section
11/11/11
Plan 9m x 9m
Memorial Hall

"The job of this institution is to inform the public. But, as a museum, do not forget to entertain and educate."

Result: Hopefully visitors can be touched and learn.

Memorial Hall
Section

"The job of this museum is to make people think and to make more responsible decisions."

Result: Regeneration Hall and hope of peace still unfulfilled.

THE RESULTING ARCHITECTURAL CONCEPT: REGENERATIVE LANDSCAPE

Please refer to "In Search of a Soul" for the process and thoughts that led to this result.

THE DESIGN PRINCIPLES

THE ARCHITECTURE: TO BOTHER VISITORS

The Canadian War Museum, from the moment of its birth, was not meant to be conventionally beautiful or to be of a conventional architectural form. The aim was to unsettle visitors somatically and to make them think and reach their own conclusions about the world and war.

THE POWER OF THE PEACE TOWER AND REMEMBRANCE DAY AT 11 A.M. (11/11/11)

The intersection of the two became even more powerful.

THE POWER OF SUN

To help honour Canadians who sacrificed and served our nation.

THE PROVISION OF ACCESS NORTH AND SOUTH

Access through the building, south and north, using the Museum to connect the Ottawa River and the pedestrian river walk to the north with the open space and public events area to the south.

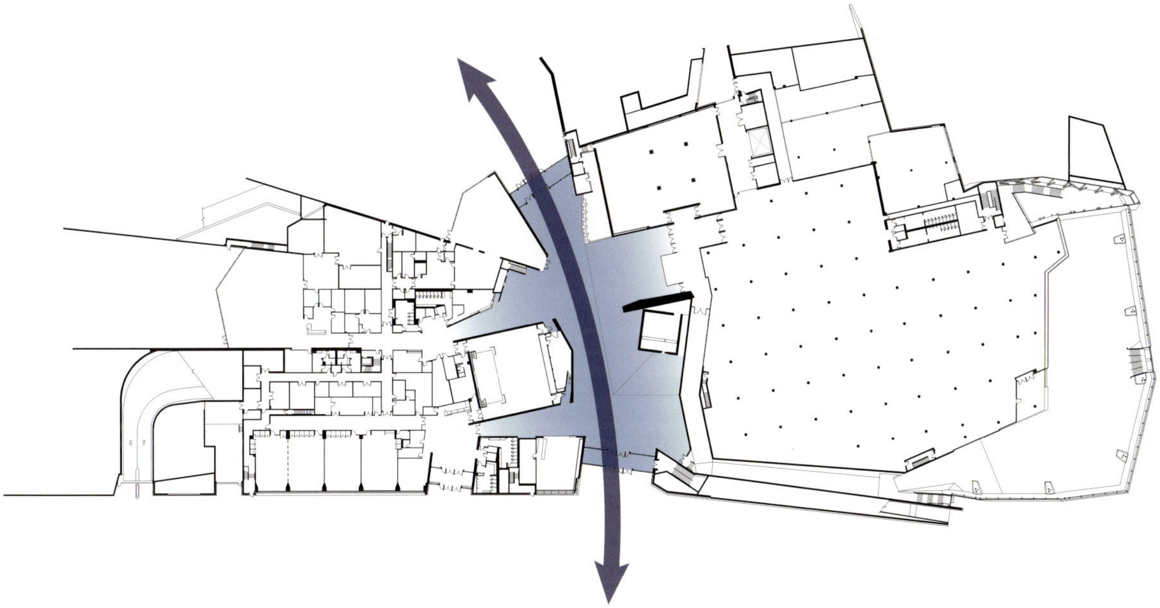

THE ORGANIZATION OF PLAN

The clearly organized separation of paying section from non-paying section at the Entrance Foyer to ease control.

ZONES

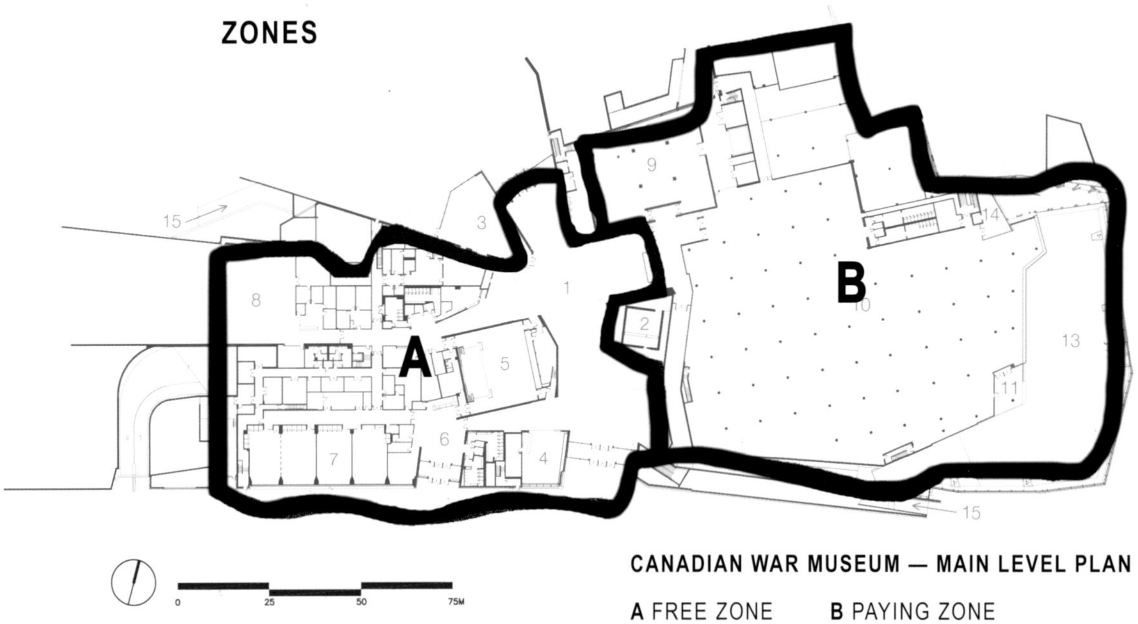

1 main lobby
2 hall of remembrance
3 cafe
4 gift shop
5 theatre
6 group entrance
7 ateliers
8 library
9 changing exhibitions
10 permanent exhibitions
11 exhibitions balcony
12 commissioners way
13 open to lebreton gallery below
14 regeneration hall mezzanine
15 la traverse

CANADIAN WAR MUSEUM — MAIN LEVEL PLAN

A FREE ZONE **B** PAYING ZONE

THE INTEGRATION WITH THE LAND AND TYING PASTORAL WEST AND URBAN EAST

The building is integrated with the land, emerging from the pastoral fields in the west and leading towards the urban centre and the Peace Tower, tying the rural quality of Ottawa to the urban core and the Parliamentary Precinct.

OUT OF THE PASTORAL WEST THE MUSEUM EMERGES SLOWLY AND QUIETLY OUT OF THE EARTH AND RISES TO ADDRESS THE URBAN CENTRE AND THE PARLIAMENTARY PRECINCT

THE GREEN ROOF

A significant part of visual concept and of sustainability.

THE TRAVERSE

The traverse over the Museum is as war trampled over ravished cities and buildings.

THE COMPACT FORM

The building form is compact and submerged for sustainability.

THE ANGULAR FORM

The angular building forms express the instability of war.

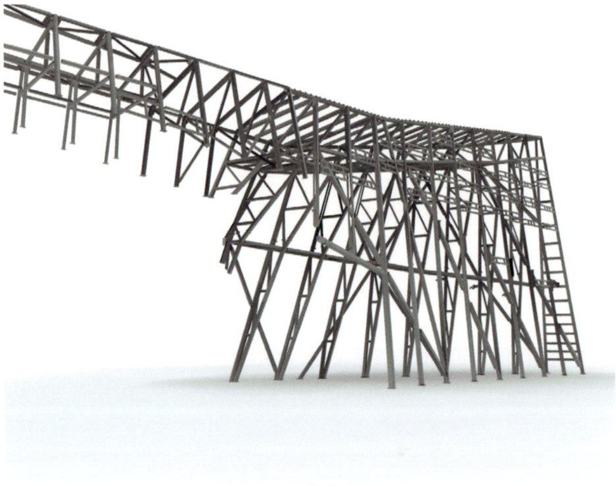

THE SIMPLE USE OF EVERYDAY CONCRETE

The building material is largely concrete, rough, utilitarian and in three patterns.

THE USE OF 15% FLY-ASH

Concrete in vertical walls has 15% fly-ash not just for economy, but to achieve the mottled appearance of aged material and wartime dilapidation.

THE HUMAN SCALE IS A MUST

THE OVERALL SENSE OF HUMANITY IS THE ESSENCE OF THE ARCHITECTURAL APPROACH

THE SOUNDS OF NATURE

The sound of nature is symbolic and conveys the message of Hope.

THE FUTURE

AN ABSOLUTE MUST TO MAINTAIN:

a. **The Purity of the Hall of Remembrance (Memorial Hall)**

b. **The Path of Sunlight on 11/11/11**

c. **"Tears of Mothers"**

Repair the "Tears of Mothers" in the Hall of Remembrance to drop a "tear" into the pool every 20 seconds, a pace of smooth breathing in meditation. This is the nation's tribute to those Canadian mothers who sacrificed their lives by sending their loved ones to war.

d. **Sound**

The Regeneration Hall and the powerful sound of nature.

e. **Less is More**

Regeneration Hall must remain uncluttered.
The maquettes of Allward should be the only display.

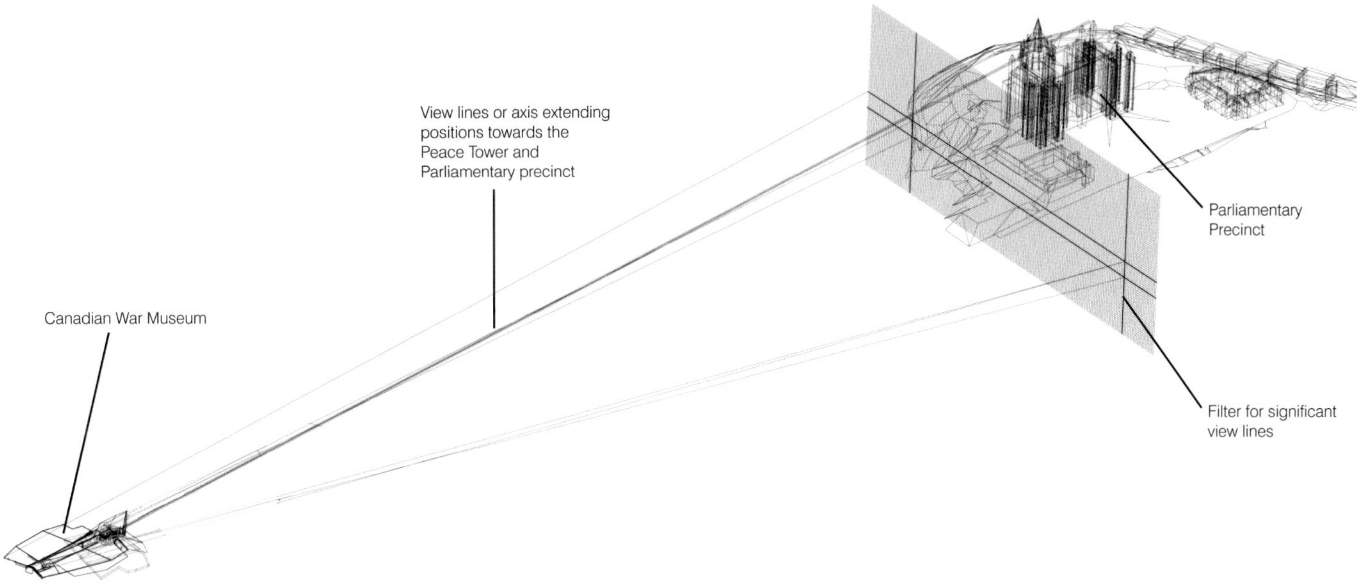

f. **The Visual Corridor**

The visual corridor between Regeneration Hall and the Peace Tower must be preserved.

g. **The Sound of Nature**

The powerful sound of a strong breeze adds emotional strength in the Regeneration Hall.

h. **The "Lest We Forget" in Regeneration Hall**

The glazed "Lest We Forget" in Morse code, in Regeneration Hall must remain.

i. **The Power of Simplicity**

Never clutter the Regeneration Hall with objects, words or signage.

j. **Access**

Maintain the free access through the War Museum foyer from the south to the north — to the Riverside Canada Trail, the islands and Chaudière Falls, and future development of exciting public and national facilities on the island.

k. **The Traverse**

Enhance the experience of First World War trenches by adding barbed wire (imitation plastic) all along the top edge.

l. The Green Roof

Keep the fox that lives nearby and seems to control the population of field mice, birds, rabbits and other creatures living in the green roof.

m. Oxidization

Let the exterior copper oxidize. In the interior, leave the beauty of the old copper from the Library of Parliament, which links time and place.

n. The Unique Stylized Morse Code Signage

o. **Minimize the Amount of Architectural Wayfinding Signage**

p. **Never Paint the Concrete**

q. **Improve Lighting in Exhibition Halls with Energy Savers**

r. **Avoid the Installation of Glazing Caps Where There Are None**

s. **Small Addition(s)**

Small addition(s) in the future should be carried out on the north side of the main structure, categorized A, B and C.

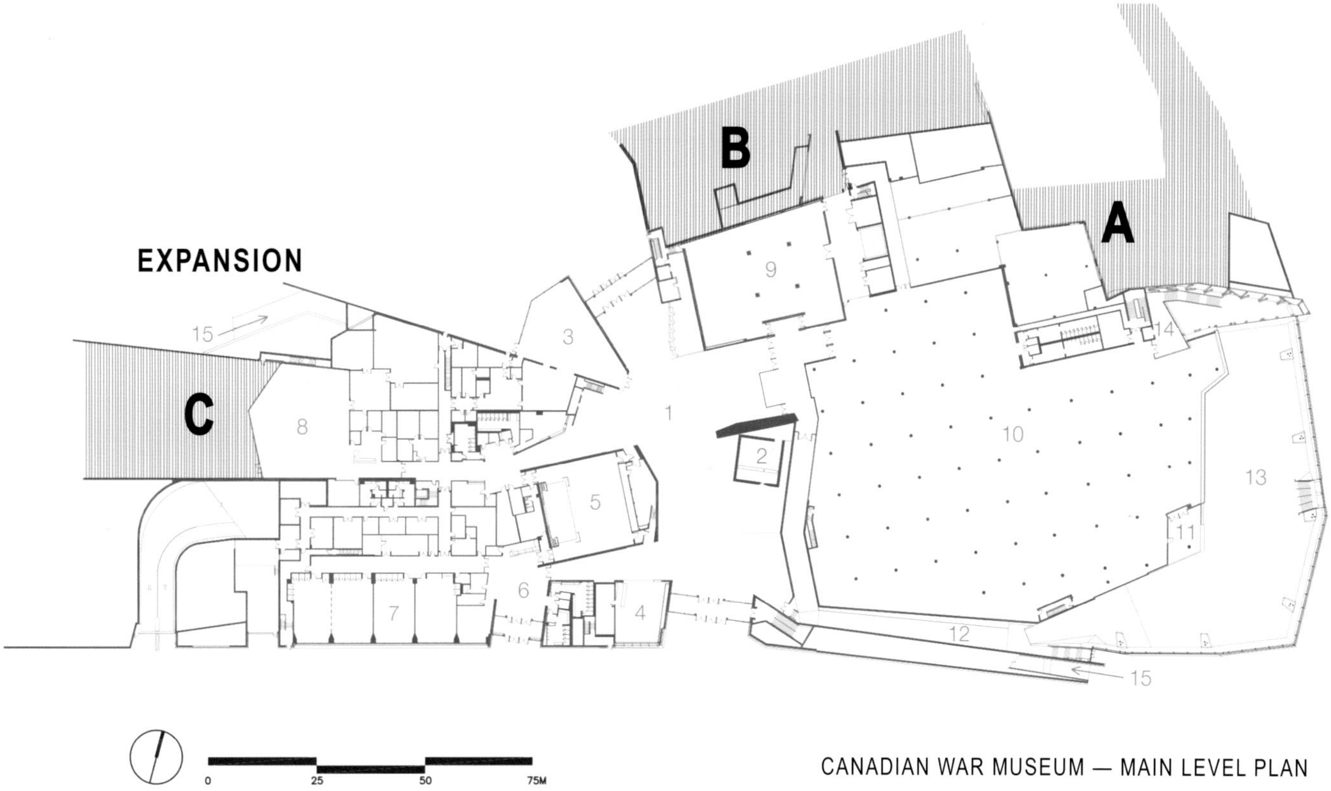

CANADIAN WAR MUSEUM — MAIN LEVEL PLAN

t. The Major Addition

A major addition should be carried out eastward to maintain balance with the original architecture. Moriyama & Teshima has already provided sketches of possibilities. There are many more that include potential gardens and outdoor exhibit areas for larger exhibits, such as a submarine and parts of battleships that the public could enter and experience. There could be areas for demonstrations such as maneuvers by tanks and other land vehicles. Another exciting possibility has recently emerged. The Holocaust Memorial Competition in 2013-14 is challenging teams from Canada and abroad to enter a competition to realize a Canadian holocaust memorial at a challenging yet amazing site at the northeast corner of Booth and Wellington adjacent to the War Museum expansion site. The winning design is to be announced early in 2014 and realized in 2016.

Thus, the future addition to the east has further challenges.

- Firstly, the view corridor between Regeneration Hall and Peace Tower must be maintained;
- The connection between the main Museum and the addition could be a wide underground passage with exhibits with natural light from above.
- Or the addition could go underground under Booth Street.
- A linkage to the Holocaust Memorial site east of Booth Street should be mandatory to the benefit of both the Memorial and Museum.

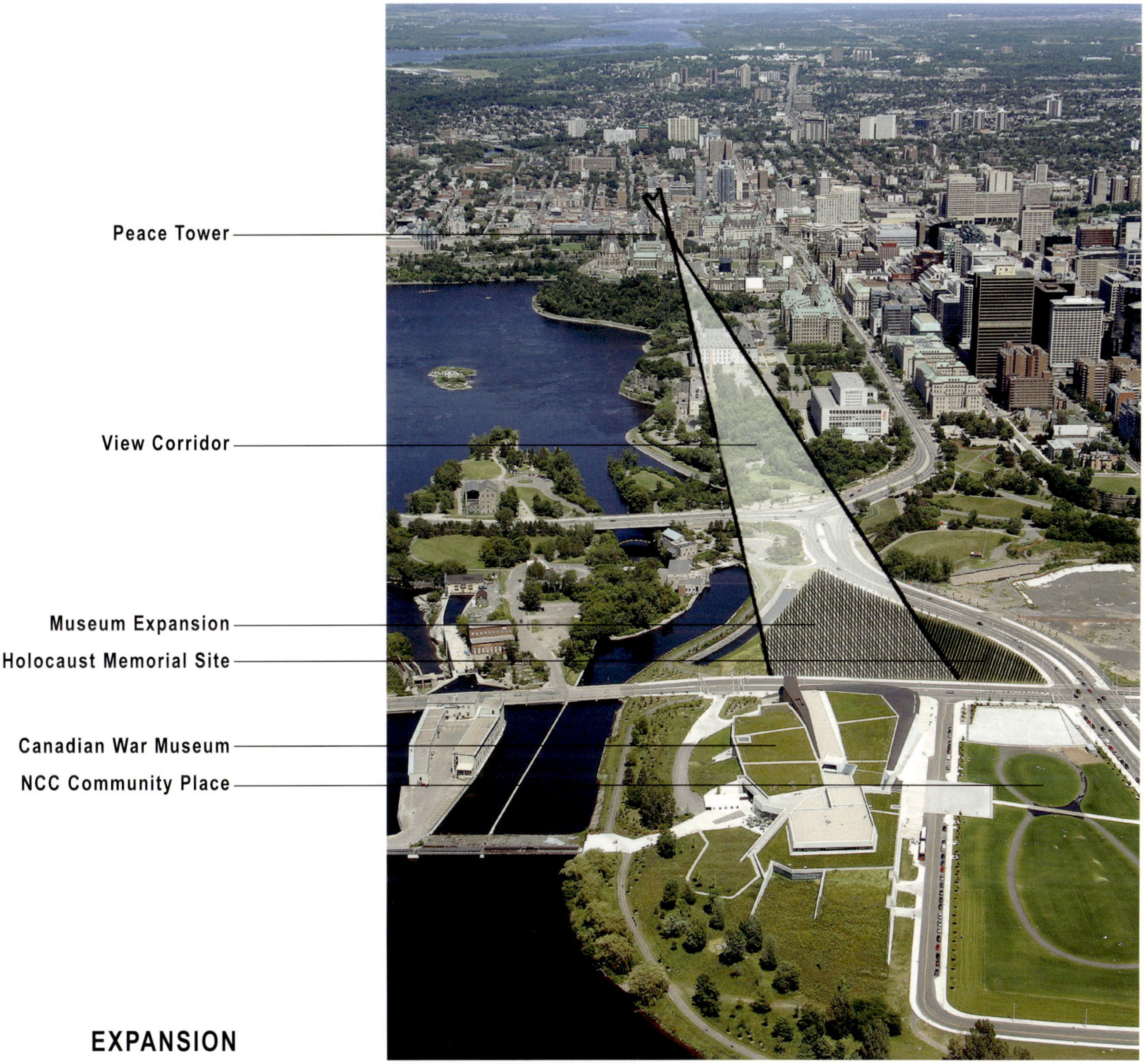
Peace Tower
View Corridor
Museum Expansion
Holocaust Memorial Site
Canadian War Museum
NCC Community Place

EXPANSION

u. **The Chimney**

The freestanding chimney in the view corridor ought to be dismantled in order to gain a purity of the connection to our democracy, represented by the Peace Tower, and our hope of world peace in Regeneration Hall.

v. **The Mezzanine**

Find meaningful use for the mezzanine above the LeBreton Gallery.

w. **Projection**

Try using projected images (movie clips of bombing or air fights, for example) on the blank wall above the LeBreton Gallery to animate the Gallery and the view from outside.

x. **Back-Projection**

Try back-projections on the frosted windows in the LeBreton Gallery to not only animate the Gallery but also act as attractions and advertising for passers-by.

y. **Caulking and Joints**

Check caulking and expansion joints for breakdown, and repair to avoid leaks.

z. **Replacement of Bulbs**

All future replacement light bulbs and fluorescent tubes must be energy conserving and warm tone in colour. Continue the use of "tank lights."

FUTURE PROJECTS TO BE CARRIED OUT

The War Museum has a complete set of As-Built Contract Documents and Specifications for reference and use.

In no order of importance, this is a list of items from the Vision and Design Disciplines that the Museum ought to carry out:

a. **The Canadian Heroes Exhibit on the Roof**
All necessary services are there. The completion of this project will give visitors, especially Canadians, ample reasons to take the Traverse to the roof of the museum. There, they can discover a wonderful exhibit of many Canadian heroes by weaving in and around the exhibition to enjoy and learn about our outstanding heroes (they need not be only war heroes). My thought was to have powerful small search lights, mounted on top of every exhibit (above 7.5 feet), shine into the night sky as a symbolic gesture to our amazing heroes and Canadian greatness, gentle but powerful, using nature's elements such as slight fog, snow fall, low clouds and mists as reflective surfaces at night. Of course, the light fixtures are not visible during the day.

LIGHTS INTO NIGHT SKY

GARDEN OF CANADIAN HEROES

b. Barbed Wire

Installation of plastic "barbed wire" across the top of the "Trench" to make the experience of Traverse and the feeling of wartime front much more lucid and memorable.

c. The Humming Mast

The Humming Mast on the Roof was eliminated during construction. It would have created magnificent heart-warming hums of nature on the roof depending on the velocity of the wind, a delicate "harp" and symbol of nature's ability to regenerate and promise life and hope. It would be a lovely tribute to Canadian modesty and courage if this design element were to be realized in the future.

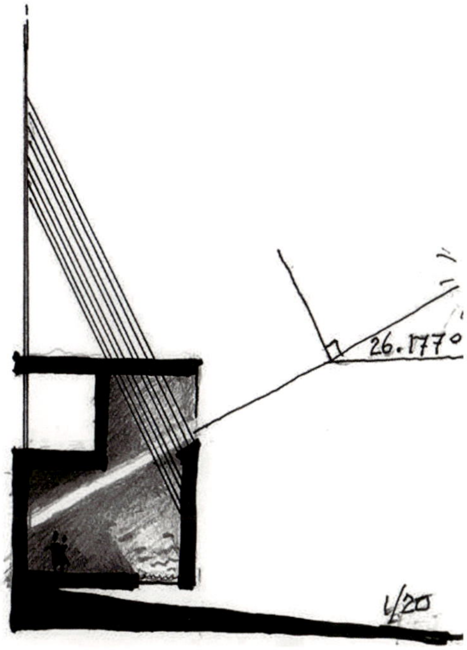

d. The Interior Slate Flooring

In the years to come, my plea is not to replace the existing slate with new slate, but to let it wear away and to let the raw concrete emerge. The process may take many years, but it will add to the graceful demise of the slate. The process will enhance the feel of decay and wartime conditions. When the slate comes near disappearing, a complete topping of concrete in triangular pattern of black, dark grey and light grey will reinforce the original vision. The design of the concrete floor layout is available in the contract documentation.

THE DREAM FOR THE FUTURE

GOLDEN CANADA EH!

I have a dream — a dream of *GOLDEN CANADA.*

When did it start?

My dream began at ages 13 and 14 in a tree house in the Rockies as a yearning of youth. I longed for my father who objected to the treatment of Japanese Canadians and was a prisoner of war in Ontario far away; I worried about my mother who, under stress, sadly lost the only baby brother I could have had; and I was experiencing the loss of freedom by forced evacuation from my own country. The yearning was intricately tied to questions I could neither understand nor answer. What is this loneliness and hopelessness that pains me? What is causing me to love nature and not some people? What is an understanding country?

These thoughts and feeling tugged my heart for many years.

Then in the late 1970s other ideas started emerging.

Why?

In 1978, our office was appointed to study the South Saskatchewan River in Saskatchewan and produce a 100 Year Plan. When our study and conceptual master plan formed the basis for the legislative creation of Meewasin Valley Authority with a mandate to realize the plan in 100 years, the thoughts of what Canada could achieve as a balanced united nation started to occupy my mind. I started asking myself, "What kind of legacy do I want to leave for my children and their children and their children?"

O'Canada

I became increasingly passionate about my dream and how to get there, especially after our involvement with the Canadian War Museum.

What?

My *GOLDEN CANADA* sees our nation taking a greater leadership role in world politics as a result of heightened confidence and balance of humanity, unrivaled civility and fuller development of complete social equality, greater economic strength, advanced educational and health priorities and achievement, fuller involvement in the North and the Arctic, together with politics of unselfish foresight and honest guts. This potential powerhouse nation could be an international influence, no longer a country representing a narrow strip that populates Canada's southern border today. *GOLDEN CANADA* will be a completely whole united nation with a clear understanding of the West and the East and a seamless integration of the North and the Arctic, not just for sovereignty rights, but for the nation's balanced economic, social, health and educational policies as rights for all citizens.

How Long?

Such an achievement may take many decades, maybe a century or more. But it is worth striving for — by starting today.

How?

How to get there is difficult, but I believe it is not impossible. I have been thinking of the strategy, the steps. It could begin with a physical starting point, an interactive centre for all Canadians and visitors to see the bigger picture of Canada, its great future potentials, and what Canada and each one of us can do to fulfill the limitless opportunities.

Where?

I have been thinking of this special place and its logical location.

I believe it should be in Ottawa, our nation's capital, in a significant spot, the location that marks the beginning of Canada, and a location that is sacred to the Aboriginal people and equally historically significant to all other Canadians. The ideal location is the island adjacent to historic Chaudière Falls.

The Place?

I have been thinking of a realizable place contained in an inexpensive architecture and nicknamed the place, *O CANADA*.

The embodiment of *O CANADA* is a "warm," symbolic *ICEBERG*, surrounded by water in summer and ice in winter, adjacent to Chaudière Falls — what a view and experience of Chaudière Falls, fully representing the beauty and power of nature and Canada.

I have designed and planned the implementation of this iconic *ICEBERG* that will stand as a living monument to Canada's individuality, progressive thinking and evolving multifaceted perspectives. Such an iceberg structure can be built inexpensively, almost "cheaply." It will glow in sunlight and its white shell with a tinge of blue will sparkle in moonlight. It will be uniquely Canada.

O CANADA will excite Canadians and enhance Canada's reputation internationally and I believe it can help as a first step and will lead us eventually to *GOLDEN CANADA*.

And, on immediate term, it will also kick-start a busy, profitable, fun community and commercial development on the Domtar site adjacent to the Canadian War Museum to the benefit of Ottawa.

O CANADA!!! O GOLDEN CANADA!!!

Can anyone share this dream?

THE USUAL SUSPECTS

IN CLOSING

I would like, firstly, to congratulate the Canadian Museum of History, Mark O'Neill and Guy Larocque for their foresight and leadership in requesting a Legacy Document for the Canadian War Museum.

Secondly, I would like to say how proud I am to have had this opportunity to carry out this assignment. I extend my thanks to Gaby Aviad and Sonia Bhogal of MTA for helping me assemble and edit this document. Of course, I dedicate this Legacy Document to Alex Rankin, the beloved leader of our Joint Venture firm, GRC, who loved the War Museum with passion and who, to my grief, passed away in the summer of 2013.

I believe this is a useful document for all those involved in the important management and maintenance of the Canadian War Museum, from the administration to the last staff member.

Moreover, I profoundly believe that a Legacy Document such as this should become a standard practice in Canada for every national institution and every important public architectural project. If such a document had been in use for the Sydney Opera House, the much publicized, often rib-tickling comical international press on the mega-mismanagement of the project as well as the extensively, expensive misguided inexperience of the Australian government could have been avoided after the discharge of its competition-winning architect. It is my sincere hope that with the help of this Legacy Document the future of managing the Canadian War Museum is more lucid, focused and efficient.

Thank you for maintaining the Vision of the Canadian War Museum and the Integrity of its architecture.

Raymond Moriyama
C.C. O.Ont. O.R.S, FRAIC, Int.FRIBA, Hon.FAIA, M.Arch.

PLEASE REFER TO “IN SEARCH OF A SOUL” BY RAYMOND MORIYAMA FOR ALL IMAGE AND WRITING CREDITS AS WELL AS PROJECT CREDITS

APPENDIX

SITE AND BUILDING BY NUMBERS

Size of site: 7.5 hectares (18.5 acres)
Footprint of building: 20,000 square metres (215,000 square feet)
Total size of building: 41,000 square metres (440,000 square Feet)
Height of building: 24.5 metres (80 feet)
Area of green roof: 16,700 square metres (180,000 square feet)
Permanent exhibition space: 5,760 square metres (62,000 square feet)
Special exhibition space: 700 square metres (7,599 square feet)
Large artifact space: 3,800 square metres (41,000 square feet)
Hall of Remembrance 81 square metres, 9m x 9m (870 square feet)
Barney Danson Theatre: 390 square metres (4,200 square feet)
The four Ateliers: 470 square metres (5,060 square feet)
Library and Archives: 1,000 square metres (11,000 square feet)
Final cost: $218.00 CAD per square foot, 2005

CONSTRUCTION BY NUMBERS

Information collected from the construction manager:
Amount of concrete: 32,000 cubic metres; weighing 106,300 tonnes
Most concrete poured in one day: 1,200 cubic metres (200 truckloads, 1,200 bucket loads)
Range of angle of sloping walls: 7 degrees to 31 degrees
Average angles of sloped floor: 3 degrees
Construction hours between start in November 2002 to completion: 1.25 million
Construction workers on site at peak: 350 to 400
Amount of steel reinforcing bars: 3,750 tonnes
Hours to build and strip forms: 189,000

AWARDS RECEIVED FOR THE CANADIAN WAR MUSEUM

Governor General's Medal 2008
Award of Excellence: Public Places & Civic Spaces
Ottawa Urban Design Award, City of Ottawa, 2005
Architectural Merit Award Cast-In-Place Concrete, 2005
Ontario Steel Design Award, Winner, 2005
Roofing Canada Award, 2005
Award for Excellence in Urban Sustainability, Globe Award, 2006
Ontario Association of Architects Award of Excellence, 2006
Royal Institute of the Architects of Ireland
  Irish Architecture Award of Excellence, 2006
Royal Institute of British Architects
RIBA International Award of Excellence, 2006
One of three finalists for the International Lubetkin Prize, 2006
LEED Gold 2006
International Leaf Award for Best Public Building Worldwide, 2006
DX Gold Award 2006

MORIYAMA'S BIO

When, to commemorate the death of the great Irish poet W. B. Yeats in 1939, fellow-poet W. H. Auden wrote "mad Ireland hurt you into poetry," he evoked not only the frequent provenance of artistic creation in human suffering, but also the power of the human spirit to transfigure and transcend suffering.

The life and architectural career of Raymond Moriyama reinforce the truth of Auden's proposition. As a dejected and rejected boy in a treehouse of his own making in an internment camp in the interior of British Columbia during the Second World War, Raymond Moriyama came to understand the intimate immensity of nature and its profound relationship to human dwelling. In the suspended solitude of the treehouse imagination augmented reality, hope and reconciliation overcame pain in the first stirrings of an architectural philosophy and practice that has embraced the eternal vernacular of wind and water, earth and sky. In creation such as the Canadian War Museum in Ottawa, the Canadian Embassy in Tokyo and the Saudi Arabian National Museum in Riyadh, Raymond Moriyama has given us architectural masterpieces imbued with spiritual values, with soul.

Raymond Moriyama's commitment to the natural world is manifested also in his efforts to protect and restore damaged ecosystems and those vulnerable to human encroachment. He and his firm have generated ground-breaking work, in naturalization and bioremediation, including the restoration of a 124 kilometre polluted Wadi Hanifa in Saudi Arabia and the Meewasin Valley Study, a 100-year Conceptual Plan for conserving the cultural and natural resources of a 60 kilometre stretch of the South Saskatchewan River Valley.

Eminent Chancellor, I present to you Raymond Moriyama, distinguished architect, renowned Canadian, friend of humanity, visionary companion of earth and sky. On behalf of the Senate and the University of Calgary, I invite you to invest him with the degree Doctor of Laws honoris causa.

June 10, 2013

This citation, composed and delivered by Brian Smith, was presented to Raymond Moriyama, his eleventh Honorary Doctorate.

Moriyama has a wife, Sachi who has given him consistency and stability, five grown children — Michi, Murina, Midori, Jason, Ajon — and ten grandchildren — Jessica, Stephanie, Steven, Mason, Jacqueline, Michael, James, Mariko, Lauren and Akiko — all of whom have contributed pride, immense joy and love, enabling him to conquer the ups and downs of the architectural and planning profession that he loves.